Strip Savvy

Strip
Savvy

2½"-Strip Quilting Designs

Kate Henderson

Martingale®
Create with Confidence

dedication

To my girls Amelia, Grace, Eva, and Olive, who are the reasons
I sew and who, thankfully, love that I sew for them.

Strip Savvy: 2½"-Strip Quilting Designs
© 2014 by Kate Henderson

Martingale®
19021 120th Ave. NE, Ste. 102
Bothell, WA 98011-9511 USA
ShopMartingale.com

Printed in China

19 18 17 16 15 14   8 7 6 5 4 3 2 1

**Library of Congress Cataloging-in-Publication Data
is available upon request.**

ISBN: 978-1-60468-375-2

Mission Statement

Dedicated to providing quality products and service to
inspire creativity.

Credits

PRESIDENT AND CEO: Tom Wierzbicki

EDITOR IN CHIEF: Mary V. Green

DESIGN DIRECTOR: Paula Schlosser

MANAGING EDITOR: Karen Costello Soltys

ACQUISITIONS EDITOR: Karen M. Burns

TECHNICAL EDITOR: Rebecca Kemp Brent

COPY EDITOR: Tiffany Mottet

PRODUCTION MANAGER: Regina Girard

COVER AND INTERIOR DESIGNER: Connor Chin

PHOTOGRAPHER: Brent Kane

ILLUSTRATOR: Lisa Lauch

contents

introduction

Living so far from my closest quilt shop, I have found precuts are a really good way to buy fabric. You know you are getting fabric that coordinates and you can try out lots of different fabrics for your money. I admit that I prefer Jelly Rolls as I love to see them stacked in a row; they look so cute and you can see a tiny glimpse of each fabric. It's so exciting when you open them and discover all the colors and patterns inside.

I save every last piece of my favorite fabrics and have found that cutting them into 2½" strips and squares is a great way to make sure I sew with them. My girls love to help me sort fabric into new and wonderful color combinations, and working this way creates some wonderfully unique quilts.

The more I play with 2½" strips of fabrics, the more possibilities I find. The options for strip quilts are endless. I hope that the patterns in this book inspire you to grab some strips or a Jelly Roll and start sewing.

general instructions

As you create your modern strip quilts, there are some basic bits of information to keep in mind. I've included my best hints and tips here. You can also visit ShopMartingale.com/HowtoQuilt for more information that's free and downloadable.

fabric

All the projects in this book are based on fabric with a 42" useable width. I used 100% cotton fabrics in every project except the second version of "Steps" on page 74, where I used scraps of many different fabrics.

Thread Tales

I use 100% cotton thread for all my piecing and quilting. I love Aurifil 50-weight thread and find it works for all aspects of quiltmaking.

Collecting 2½" Strips

The easiest way to get 2½" strips for your project is to buy them precut. Moda and other fabric companies package precut 2½" strips of their lines. Moda Jelly Rolls usually include 40 strips, which is perfect for a lot of projects in this book. Check the label to determine how many strips are included in a specific roll or bundle of strips.

There are lots of other ways to get 2½" strips. When I buy a length of fabric, I always cut off a 2½" strip and add it to my collection. If you like to buy fat quarters, cut two strips, 2½" wide, along the width of the fat quarter (21") and you will have the equivalent of one full-width strip. Each square in a Moda Layer Cake can be cut into four strips, 2½" x 10".

To use scraps in strip quilts, go through your scrap stash and cut small scraps into 2½" squares or 2½" x 4½" rectangles. Cut larger scraps into 2½"

strips. Organize and store the cut pieces so they are ready to go when you're ready to sew.

If you're not sure where to start with a scrappy quilt or you're unsure about choosing a color theme, start with a few selections from the same fabric line and then add other pieces with coordinating colors and shapes. Don't overthink; just grab what catches your eye first.

A couple of quilts in this book use 42 strips of fabric, which is more than the contents of a single Jelly Roll. Rather than buying a second Jelly Roll, purchase a little extra binding or backing fabric and cut the needed strips from them, or use strips from your stash.

Fabric Preparation and Storage

Jelly Rolls should not be prewashed; putting one into the washing machine will just result in a tangled mess of fabric. I no longer prewash any of my fabric, and haven't had any disasters when washing my quilts for the first time. I do add a dye catcher to the washing machine, especially if the quilt includes dark or red fabrics, as they sometimes run or bleed excess dye.

Jelly Rolls and fabric strips will often have a strong crease where they are folded in half. Unfold and press each strip so it's flat when cut, but take care not to distort the strip as you press.

There are many ways to store 2½" strips. I like to store my 2½" squares and 2½" x 4½" rectangles in large, clear cookie jars that let me see the contents. I try to keep long strips in a tub, neatly folded or wound, but I admit that, more often than I like, they end up tangled and I have to dig through to find what I want. Find a system that works for you; sort either by size or by color and use baskets or plastic tubs.

Background Fabrics

The background fabric you choose can really change the look of your quilt. Solids, especially white or cream, are always a go-to option for me. I tend to use a lot of brighter colors; a white background makes them pop and provides a nice contrast to the fabrics in the blocks. A really dark-gray fabric can do the same. I love the look of shot cottons (woven from two different cotton thread colors, one for the warp and one for the weft) for backgrounds, and they are especially lovely in quilts where there is a lot of negative space.

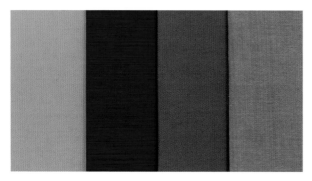

Shot cottons are good background choices.

If you want to branch out a little, choose a fabric with a small spot motif or dots. Be sure there is good contrast between the strip fabrics and the background.

A mostly solid fabric with a single print motif can be used as a background.

Monochromatic prints are another good choice for backgrounds. They often look like solid fabrics from a distance, but add interest and texture close up.

Monochromatic and textured prints are good background choices.

rotary cutting

You'll need to do some cutting even when a project begins with precuts, and rotary cutting is the easiest and most accurate method. Most of the projects in this book use basic square and rectangular rotary-cutting rulers. Having rulers of various sizes will simplify the cutting process, but you can manage with just a couple of lengths. I find it worth investing in a ruler and mat at least 24" long to make cutting strips from the width of the fabric very easy.

The only other rulers used for these projects are a 45° triangle for the "Reflections" quilt on page 75 and a 45° Half-Square Triangle ruler from Creative Grids for the half-square-triangle units in "Night Sky" on page 63. Even these two rulers are optional.

Lefties Take Note

Reverse the following rotary-cutting instructions if you are left-handed.

If you're cutting your own strips from yardage, fold the fabric in half with the selvages aligned and place it on a cutting mat with the folded edge closest to you. Straighten one fabric edge by aligning a ruler line with the fold and cutting perpendicular to the fold. Turn the mat and fabric 180° to position them for cutting strips.

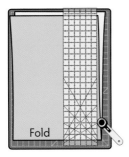

To cut a strip of the desired width, align the ruler marking for that width with the trimmed edge of the fabric and cut along the right-hand edge of the ruler.

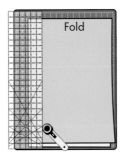

Trim the selvages from the ends of the strip and it's ready for crosscutting into squares and rectangles.

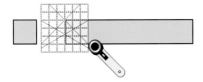

A couple of projects in this book require you to cut squares into triangles. Once you have cut the specified square, cut it in half diagonally from corner to corner for half-square triangles. Cut diagonally from all four corners for quarter-square triangles.

Half-square triangles

Quarter-square triangles

seam allowances

A ¼"-wide seam allowance is used throughout this book. Even if you use a ¼" presser foot on your machine, it's worth checking to make sure you're sewing an accurate ¼"-wide seam allowance. A 60"-wide quilt made from 2½" strips has many seams, and by the end you could be off by quite a bit!

To check your seam allowance, sew three 2½"-wide strips together and press. The finished unit should measure 6½" wide. If it measures more than 6½", increase the seam allowances by a thread's width (0.5 mm) or two. If it measures less than 6½", make the seam allowances correspondingly narrower. Keep testing until your seam allowance is exactly ¼" wide.

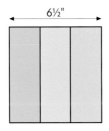
6½"

pressing

Seam allowances can be pressed to one side or open. My only rule for pressing seam allowances is to do what you prefer. I tend to do a bit of both, and throughout this book, I indicate the pressing direction for each seam allowance.

I press seam allowances open in most of my blocks, especially when there are triangle or half-square corners. I think it makes for a flatter quilt top and more precise matching of seams. If there is sashing in the quilt, I press the seam allowances to one side, toward the sashing. In quilts with mainly straight lines or simple quilts I want to make quickly, I press the seam allowances to one side.

quick piecing techniques

After you cut the pieces, it's time to sew them together! Here are two techniques to make your piecing faster and more accurate.

Strip Piecing

Strip piecing is a great way to save time when you're making identical units from 2½" strips. To strip piece, sew the strips together along their long edges, and then crosscut into units of the required shape and size. Cutting the units after you have sewn the strips together can be more accurate than piecing individual 2½" squares.

Chain Piecing

Chain piecing saves time and thread. Instead of sewing just two pieces of fabric together at a time, get a whole pile ready to sew. After you have sewn the first pair, leave the presser foot down, feed the next pair under the foot, and keep sewing. When all the pieces in the pile are sewn, lift the presser foot, cut the thread, and then cut the chains of thread between each pair.

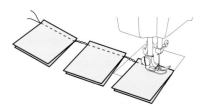

special piecing techniques

Triangle corners (sometimes called folded corners), half-square-triangle units, and flying-geese units are used in many of the patterns in this book. Here are some special sewing techniques that can speed up the process of making many of these units.

Triangle Corners

1 With a sharp pencil, draw a diagonal line from corner to corner across the wrong side of a 2½" square. Place the square at one end of a 2½" strip, right sides together, and sew one thread-width away from the drawn line on the seam-allowance side.

2 Fold the resulting triangle over the seam line to check that it matches the edges of the 2½" strip and adjust the stitching line if necessary. Return the square to the sewing position and trim the corner, leaving a ¼"-wide seam allowance. Fold the resulting triangle outward and press the seam allowances open.

To save time drawing lines on the many 2½" squares required for some patterns, place a strip of masking tape on the sewing machine bed as a guide for positioning the squares. Start sewing at the outer corner and align the square's opposite corner with the edge of the masking tape.

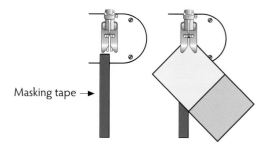

Masking tape →

Half-Square-Triangle Units

To make half-square-triangle units from two 2½" squares, follow the instructions for triangle corners using the second 2½" square in place of the 2½"-wide strip.

I used a special ruler to make the half-square-triangle units in "Night Sky" on page 63. The 45° Half-Square Triangle ruler by Creative Grids makes cutting and sewing half-square triangles easy and saves fabric.

Flying-Geese Units

1 Each flying-geese unit uses two 2½" squares and a 2½" x 4½" rectangle. Draw diagonal lines from corner to corner across the wrong sides of both squares.

2 Place a square on one end of the rectangle, right sides together, and sew one thread-width away from the drawn line on the seam-allowance side.

3 Fold the triangle over the seam line to check that it matches the edges of the rectangle and adjust the stitching line if necessary. Return the square to the sewing position and trim the corner, leaving a ¼"-wide seam allowance. Fold the resulting triangle outward and press the seam allowances open.

4 Repeat steps 2 and 3 to add the second square to the other end of the rectangle. Be sure to orient the seam lines to form a large triangle in the middle of the unit.

Adjusting Quilt Sizes

Most of the quilts in this book can be made smaller or larger by eliminating or adding rows. To make a bigger quilt, grab more strips and keep sewing blocks until you have the quilt size you want. If the quilt has a border, remember to cut the border strips longer, piecing them if necessary. If the quilt has no borders, just increase the sizes of the batting and backing to accommodate the new blocks.

adding borders

Sometimes a quilt design can be enhanced by adding a border. A busy quilt sometimes needs a simple border, while a simple quilt may benefit from an interesting pattern in the border. A border can also echo the central quilt design. Simple but very effective borders can be made with leftover scraps from Jelly Rolls and other 2½" strips.

Wall Wisdom

If you're unsure whether or not your quilt needs a border, play with options on a design wall. I made mine by simply hanging a piece of batting on the wall, but there are many tutorials online for making one. You can arrange the quilt pieces on the design wall before you even begin sewing to determine if the project needs a border.

The border ideas below all use simple piecing or techniques that are described in this book such as triangle corners and flying-geese units. The border blocks each finish to either 2", 4", or 8" wide, making them easy to add to quilts pieced from 2½"-wide strips.

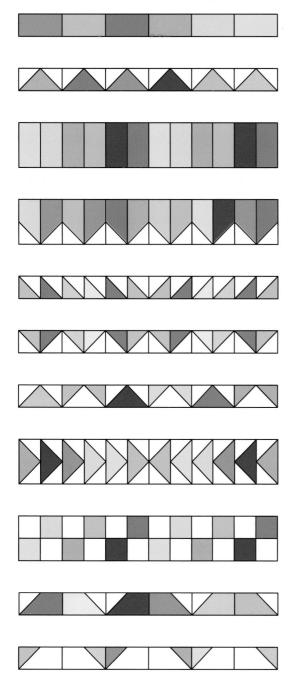

Within this book, the exact measurements for sashing and borders are given in each project's instructions, but it's always a good idea to measure the quilt before attaching the borders to ensure that the quilt lies flat and straight. Measure the length of the pieced quilt top from raw edge to raw edge in two different places and average the measurements. Cut the side borders this length, which includes a ½" seam allowance. Mark the centers of the quilt top and borders. Sew the borders in place, matching the center point and both ends. Press the seam allowances as directed.

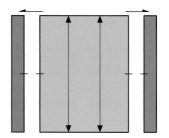

Measure the length in two places; match the centers.

Measure the width of the quilt top, including the side borders, in the same way. Cut and attach the borders as before. Press the seam allowances as directed.

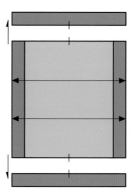

Include the borders in the width measurement.

If measuring reveals that a pieced border is slightly too big or too small it can be easily fixed. If the border is too large, sew a larger seam allowance between one or two border blocks. Measure again and repeat if necessary. If the border is too small, remove stitches and make one or two seam allowances a bit narrower to compensate.

quilting the quilt

When the piecing is complete, you will need to add backing and batting for loft and to finish the wrong side of the quilt.

Backing

The backing measurements in each project allow at least 3" beyond the quilt top on all sides. For most of the quilts in this book you will have to piece the backing.

Remove the selvages from the fabric and cut the purchased piece in half across the fabric width. Align the lengthwise edges of the two pieces, right sides together, and sew with a ½" seam. Press the seam allowances open.

Which Way?

The backing seam can run horizontally or vertically across the quilt. The instructions give the minimum possible yardage for the backing, which may mean that its lengthwise grain runs across the width of the quilt. If you prefer a vertical seam, recalculate the yardage and purchase more fabric if necessary.

To make a more interesting backing, you can incorporate leftover strips from the quilt top or make extra blocks to stitch into the backing. Use your imagination and make the backing as interesting as the front!

Batting

I use 100% cotton batting in my quilts. I machine quilt them all on a domestic machine and find cotton batting easy to manage. I also like the low-loft look of cotton batting and live in a climate where really warm quilts aren't needed. Cotton batting is easy to machine wash and dry, which is important in my house; we use the quilts all the time, and my children play on and build cubbies with them.

Different types of batting create slightly different looks when quilted, so experiment with several and use the one you prefer.

Basting

To baste the quilt, spread out the backing, wrong side up, on a flat surface such as a table (or two placed side by side) or on the floor. I have a wooden floor and always baste my quilts there. Smooth the backing until it's flat and secure the edges to the floor or table with masking tape. Center the batting over the backing, smoothing out any wrinkles. Center the quilt top over the batting, right side up, and smooth into place.

If you will be machine quilting, baste the layers together by placing safety pins every 3" to 4" through all the layers. I find it best to start in the middle and work toward the edges. Other basting methods include long hand-basting stitches and basting sprays. Choose the one that works best for your quilting preferences.

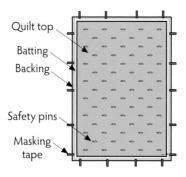

Quilt top
Batting
Backing
Safety pins
Masking tape

Quilting

I like to machine quilt all my own quilts on a normal, domestic sewing machine. There is something magical about seeing a quilt top transform into a quilt, and I'm always so impatient to see a quilt finished! I don't have to wait if I do the quilting myself. You can quilt in straight lines using a walking foot, employ free-motion techniques, or use a combination of both as I do. I've included a description of my quilting at the end of each project.

If you are new to machine quilting, a good place to start is sewing straight lines that follow the lines of the quilt. I like to use the edge of my walking foot as a guide to stitching along both sides of a seam, positioning the quilting about 1" apart. Test different stitch lengths on your machine when using a walking foot; I find my stitches look best when they are slightly longer than my piecing stitches.

Simple meandering lines make a good introduction to free-motion quilting. Lower or cover the machine's feed dogs and use a darning foot or one specifically meant for free-motion quilting. Make a mini quilt from fabric and batting scraps to practice on before working on a big quilt; free-motion quilting becomes easier with practice. When you're satisfied with your meandering lines, try adding loops and flowers as you quilt.

Bubble quilting

Serpentine stitches are a great alternative to ordinary straight stitches.

Flower quilting

binding

I make different types of bindings, either from a variety of scraps or a single fabric. For either type, I cut strips across the fabric width rather than on the bias. I machine stitch the binding from the front of the quilt, fold it over the raw edges, and hand sew it to the backing.

Scrappy Binding

The great thing about making quilts with 2½" strips is that those strips are also the perfect width for binding; it's so easy to collect the scraps of strips and sew them together for the binding. I sew my scraps together end to end to minimize waste and I prefer this look to diagonal seams when I am using scraps.

Use a ¼"-wide seam allowance and press the seam allowances open to minimize bulk. Before attaching the binding to the quilt, try to make sure none of the seams end up on the quilt corners where the extra bulk makes sewing the binding difficult.

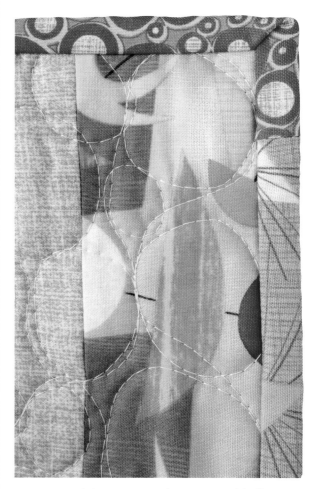

Use straight seams to piece scrappy bindings.

One-Fabric Binding

Remove the selvages from the binding strips and sew them together with diagonal seams as shown. Trim the excess fabric, leaving a ¼"-wide seam allowance, and press the seam allowances open.

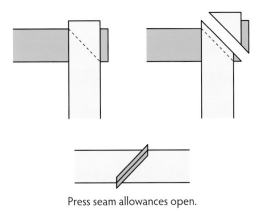

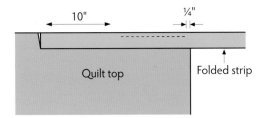

Press seam allowances open.

Attaching the Binding

1 Fold the binding strip in half lengthwise, wrong sides together, and press.

2 Trim the batting and backing to match the quilt top. Using a walking foot and a ¼"-wide seam allowance, start sewing the binding to the quilt, leaving about 10" of binding unstitched at the start. Stop sewing ¼" before the corner and backstitch.

10"   ¼"

Quilt top   Folded strip

3 Position the quilt for sewing the second side. Fold the binding up and then back down on itself, aligning the raw edges with the second side of the quilt. Stitch the binding to the second side of the quilt with a ¼"-wide seam allowance, stopping and backstitching ¼" before the next corner. Repeat around the quilt. Finish sewing 5" to 6" from the beginning of the stitching and take the quilt out of the machine.

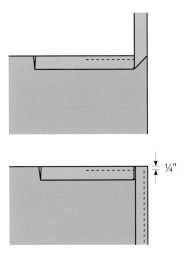

¼"

4 To join a one-fabric binding, lay the ends of the binding strip on top of each other and trim, leaving a 2½" overlap. Unfold the binding ends and position them right sides together and at right angles, as you did when joining the binding strips. Pin the pieces in place and sew from corner to corner. Trim the excess fabric, leaving a ¼"-wide seam allowance.

2½" overlap

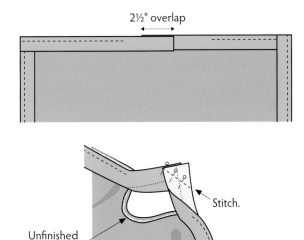

Unfinished quilt edge

Stitch.

5 If you are using a scrappy binding, lay the binding
ends on top of each other and trim, leaving a ½"
overlap. Unfold the ends of the binding and, with right
sides together, sew the ends with a ¼"-wide seam
allowance.

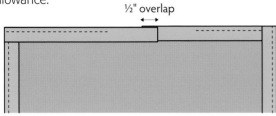

½" overlap

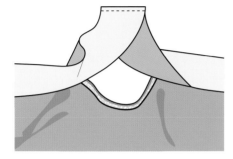

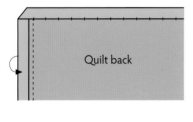

Stitch ends together.

6 For either method, finger-press the seam open,
refold the binding, and finish sewing it to the
quilt. Fold the binding to the back of the quilt, covering
the raw edges, and hand stitch it in place, mitering the
corners.

Quilt back

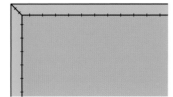

Quilts with Borders

Sometimes a border, pieced or plain, is the perfect complement to the quilt design. Consider making your borders from leftover squares and rectangles.

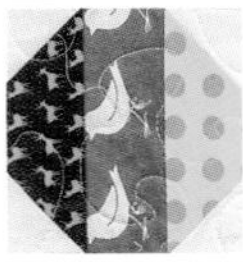

snowball explosion

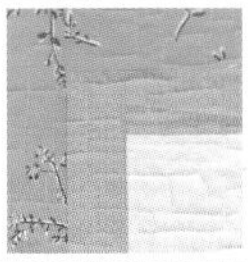

open sesame

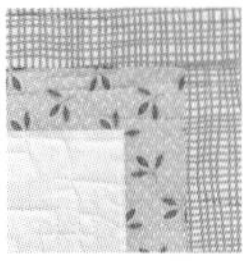

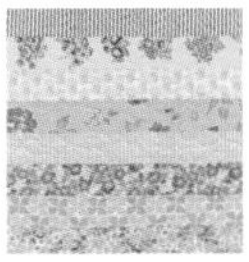

summer picnic

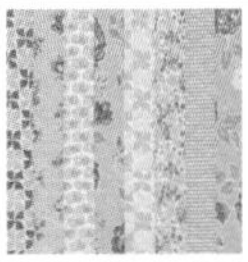

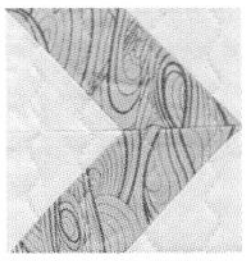

kaleidoscope

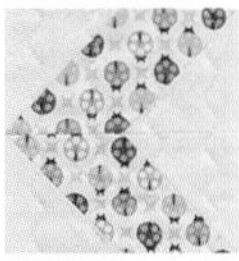

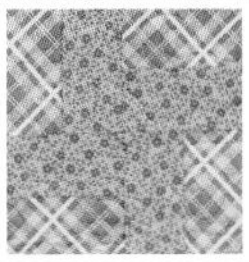

wind farm

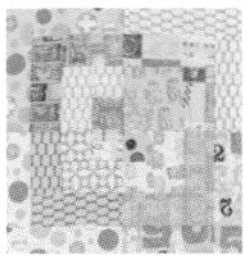

round and round

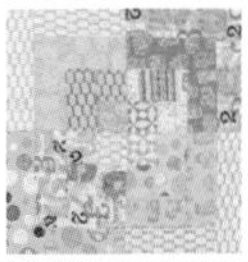

little houses

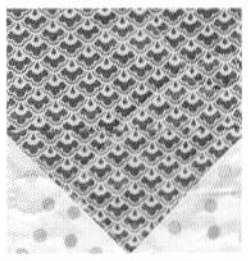

snowball explosion

These Striped Snowball blocks are easy to make. The strip piecing creates a secondary pattern that rises above the ordinary.

materials

Yardage is based on 42"-wide fabric.

40 strips, 2½" x 42", of assorted bright prints for blocks and borders

1⅞ yards of white solid for blocks and borders

½ yard of brown print for binding

3 yards of fabric for backing

54" x 66" piece of batting

cutting

From *each* of 36 print strips, cut:
1 strip, 2½" x 27" (36 total)
2 rectangles, 2½" x 4½" (72 total)

From *each* of the remaining 4 print strips, cut:
5 rectangles, 2½" x 4½" (20 total)

From the white solid, cut:
19 strips, 2½" x 42"; crosscut into 284 squares, 2½" x 2½"
5 strips, 2½" x 42"
1 strip, 4½" x 42"; crosscut into 4 squares, 4½" x 4½"

From the brown print, cut:
6 strips, 2½" x 42"

making the blocks

1 Organize the 2½" x 27" strips into 12 piles of three strips each. Sew each group of rectangles together along their long edges and press the seam allowances open. Cut four squares, 6½" x 6½", from each strip set.

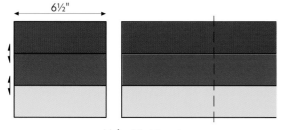

6½"

Make 12 strip sets.
Cut 4 squares from each.

2 Referring to "Triangle Corners" on page 12, use the white 2½" squares to add a triangle to each corner of the pieced squares. Make 48.

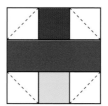 

Make 48.

assembling the quilt

1 Arrange the blocks in eight rows of six blocks each, rotating every other block as shown. Sew the blocks together in rows and press the seam allowances open. Sew the rows together and press the seam allowances open.

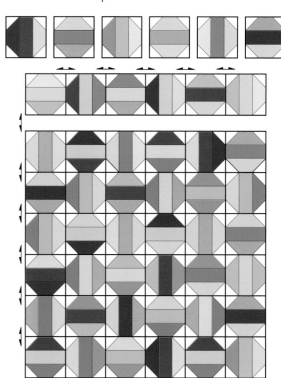

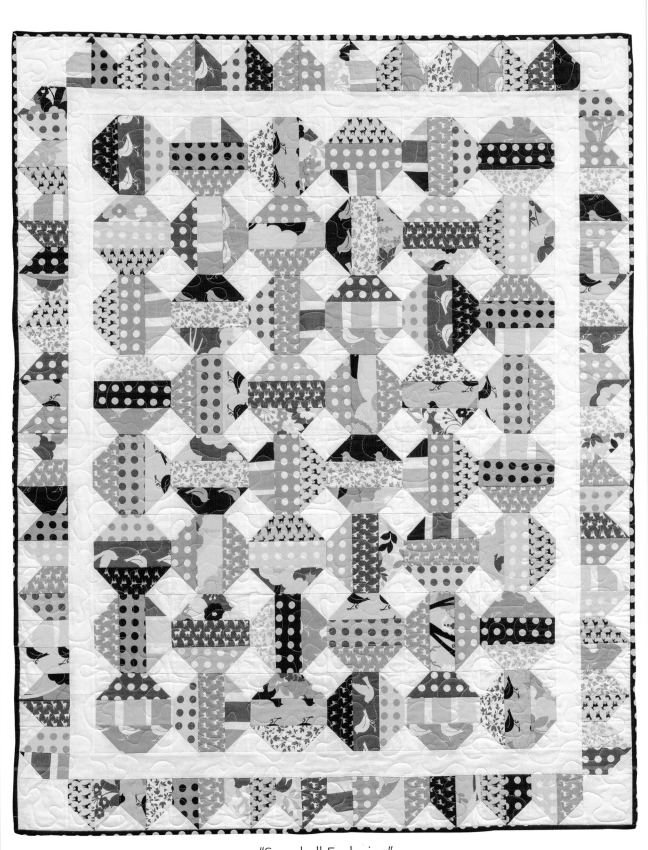

"Snowball Explosion"

Pieced and quilted by Kate Henderson

Finished quilt: 48" x 60"

Finished block: 6" x 6"

2 Sew three white 2½" x 42" strips together end to end. From the pieced strip, cut two inner borders 48½" long. From the two remaining white strips, cut two inner borders 40½" long.

3 Sew the 48½"-long inner borders to the sides of the quilt. Press the seam allowances toward the borders. Sew the 40½"-long inner borders to the top and bottom of the quilt. Press the seam allowances toward the borders.

4 Referring to "Triangle Corners," use the print rectangles and remaining white 2½" squares to make triangle-corner units as shown. Make 46 each of units A and B. Press the seam allowances open.

Unit A.
Make 46.

Unit B.
Make 46.

5 Sew the A and B units together in pairs as shown. Press the seam allowances open.

6 Sew 13 of the units from step 5 together to make a side border; make two. Sew 10 units together to make the top border; add a white 4½" square to each end. Repeat to make the bottom border. Press the seam allowances open.

7 Sew the side borders to the quilt and press the seam allowances toward the inner border. Sew the top and bottom borders to the quilt and press the seam allowances toward the inner border.

finishing the quilt

1 Layer the quilt top, batting, and backing; baste the layers together. Quilt as desired. I free-motion quilted a meandering pattern.

2 Referring to "Binding" on page 17, use the brown strips to bind the edges of the quilt. Add a label if desired.

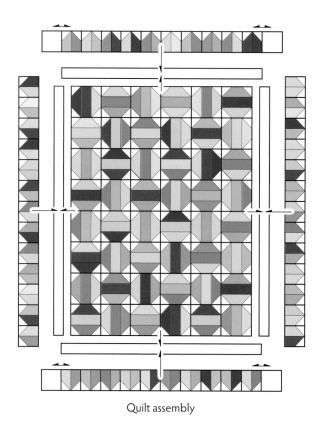

Quilt assembly

open sesame

A simple inner border provides a frame for the quilt's center design, while the outer border adds width and color.

materials

Yardage is based on 42"-wide fabric.

42 strips, 2½" x 42", of assorted bold prints for blocks and borders

1⅜ yards of white solid for the blocks and borders

⅝ yard of gray print for binding

3¾ yards of fabric for backing

62" x 70" piece of batting

cutting

From *each* of the 42 print strips, cut:
- 1 rectangle, 2½" x 8½" (42 total)
- 2 rectangles, 2½" x 6½" (84 total)
- 3 rectangles, 2½" x 4½" (126 total; 28 will be left over)

From the white solid, cut:
- 6 strips, 4½" x 42"; crosscut into 42 squares, 4½" x 4½"
- 6 strips, 2½" x 42"

From the gray print, cut:
- 7 strips, 2½" x 42"

making the blocks

1 Sew a print 2½" x 4½" rectangle to one side of a white square. Press the seam allowances open. Sew a matching print 2½" x 6½" rectangle to the top of the unit and press the seam allowances open.

2 Sew a contrasting print 2½" x 6½" rectangle to the side of the unit from step 1. Press the seam allowances open. Sew a matching 2½" x 8½" rectangle to the top of the unit and press the seam allowances open. Make 42.

Make 42.

assembling the quilt

1 Arrange the blocks in seven rows of six blocks each, rotating alternate blocks as shown. Sew the blocks together in rows and press the seam allowances open. Sew the rows together and press the seam allowances open.

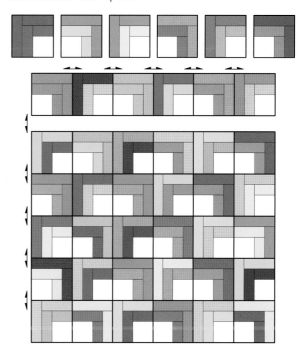

"Open Sesame"

| Pieced and quilted by Kate Henderson | **Finished quilt:** 56" x 64" | **Finished block:** 8" x 8" |

2 Sew three of the white strips together end to end. From the pieced strip, cut two inner borders 56½" long. Sew the remaining three white strips together end to end. From the pieced strip, cut two inner borders 52½" long and four squares, 2½" x 2½", to be used for the outer border.

3 Sew the 56½"-long inner borders to the sides of the quilt. Press the seam allowances toward the borders. Sew the 52½"-long strips to the top and bottom of the quilt and press the seam allowances toward the borders.

4 Sew 15 of the remaining 2½" x 4½" rectangles together end to end to make a side border; make two and press the seam allowances open. Sew 13 of the remaining 2½" x 4½" rectangles together for the

top border; repeat to make the bottom border. Sew a white 2½" square from step 2 to each end of the top and bottom borders.

5 Sew the side borders to the quilt and press the seam allowances toward the inner border. Sew the top and bottom borders to the quilt and press the seam allowances toward the inner border.

finishing the quilt

1 Layer the quilt top, batting, and backing; baste the layers together. Quilt as desired. I free-motion quilted overlapping squares and rectangles.

2 Referring to "Binding" on page 17, use the gray strips to bind the edges of the quilt. Add a label if desired.

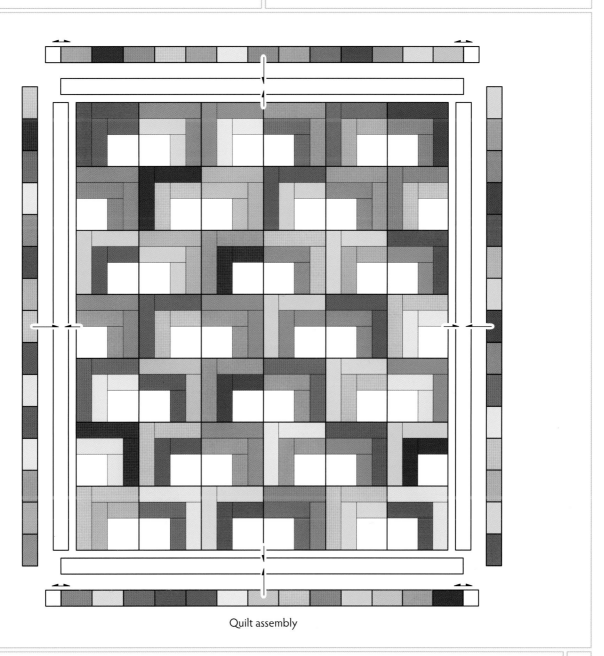

Quilt assembly

summer picnic

We have a lovely weeping mulberry tree in front of our house which the children think is magical. I think this quilt is the perfect blanket for the picnics they have underneath their magical tree.

materials

Yardage is based on 42"-wide fabric.

40 strips, 2½" x 42", of assorted prints for blocks and borders

1¼ yards of white-with-red pindot for borders

⅝ yard of red print for binding

3⅞ yards of fabric for backing

66" x 66" piece of batting

cutting

From *each* of 32 print strips, cut:
2 rectangles, 2½" x 16½" (64 total)

From *each* of 7 print strips, cut:
1 rectangle, 2½" x 16½" (7 total)

From the remaining print strip, cut:
1 rectangle, 2½" x 16½"
4 squares, 2½" x 2½"

From the scraps of the print strips, cut:
28 rectangles, 2½" x 8½"

From the white-with-red pindot, cut:
6 strips, 4½" x 42"
4 strips, 2½" x 42"; crosscut into 56 squares, 2½" x 2½"

From the red print, cut:
7 strips, 2½" x 42"

Careful Cutting

Cut carefully, as you will use almost the full width of the strips.

making the blocks

Sew eight assorted print 2½" x 16½" rectangles together along their long edges to form a 16½" square. Make nine.

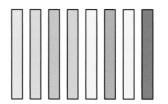 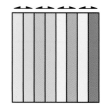

Make 9.

assembling the quilt

1 Arrange the blocks in three rows of three blocks each, rotating every other block as shown. Sew the blocks together in rows and press the seam allowances open. Sew the rows together and press the seam allowances open.

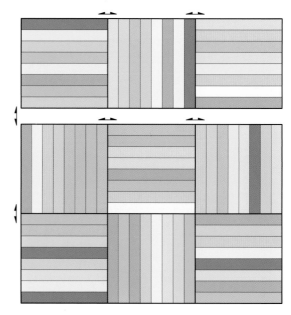

2 Sew three pindot strips together end to end. From the pieced strip, cut two inner borders 48½" long. Sew the three remaining pindot strips together end to end and cut two inner borders 56½" long.

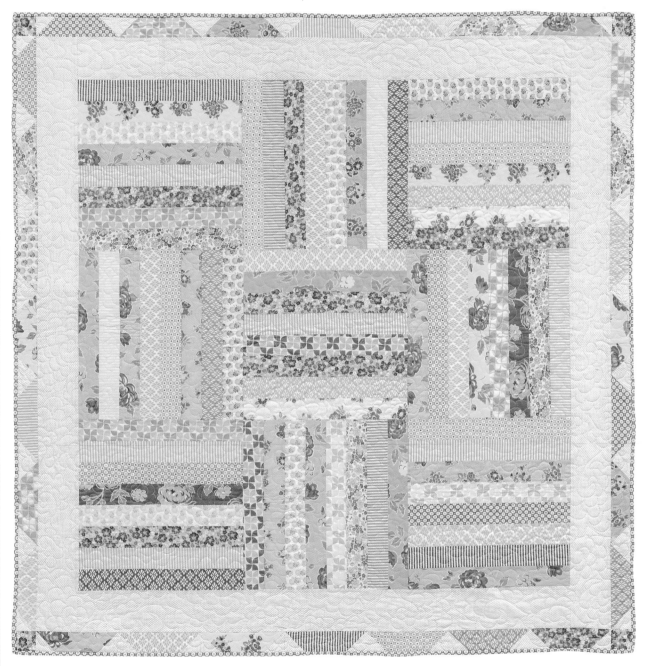

"Summer Picnic"

Pieced and quilted by Kate Henderson | **Finished quilt:** 60" x 60" | **Finished block:** 16" x 16"

3 Sew the 48½"-long inner borders to the sides of the quilt. Press the seam allowances toward the borders. Sew the 56½"-long inner borders to the top and bottom of the quilt. Press the seam allowances toward the borders.

4 Referring to "Triangle Corners" on page 12, use pindot squares to make a triangle corner at each end of a print 2½" x 8½" rectangle. Make 28.

Make 28.

5 Sew together seven of the units from step 4 to make one outer border. Make four.

Make 4.

6 Sew an outer border to each side of the quilt top and press the seam allowances toward the inner border. Sew a print 2½" square to each end of the remaining outer borders. Sew these outer borders to the top and bottom of the quilt and press the seam allowances toward the inner border.

finishing the quilt

1 Layer the quilt top, batting, and backing; baste the layers together. Quilt as desired. I free-motion quilted an all-over flower pattern.

2 Referring to "Binding" on page 17, use the red strips to bind the edges of the quilt. Add a label if desired.

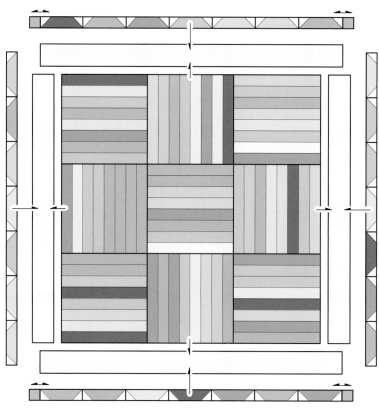

Quilt assembly

kaleidoscope

As a child I thought kaleidoscopes were magical. This quilt reminds me of looking through one.

materials

Yardage is based on 42"-wide fabric.

29 strips, 2½" x 42", of assorted prints for blocks and borders

1½ yards of cream solid for blocks and borders

½ yard of green print for binding

2¾ yards of fabric for backing

46" x 50" piece of batting

cutting

From *each* of the 29 print strips, cut:
    7 rectangles, 2½" x 4½" (203 total; 21 will be left over)

From the cream solid, cut:
    13 strips, 2½" x 42"; crosscut into 208 squares, 2½" x 2½"*
    4 strips, 2½" x 42"; crosscut into four strips, 2½" x 36½"

From the green print, cut:
    5 strips, 2½" x 42"

*If your fabric is slightly narrower, cut up to two additional strips to achieve the right number of squares.

Variety Is the Spice

All the necessary print rectangles can be cut from just 21 strips, but I wanted more variety, so I used 29 different fabric strips.

making the blocks

1 Referring to "Triangle Corners" on page 12, use two matching print rectangles and four cream squares to make a pair of double triangle-corner units as shown. You will be stitching in different directions for each unit to construct a mirror-image pair. Press the seam allowances open. Make 32 pairs (64 total).

2 Sew the two units from step 1 together. Press the seam allowances open. Make 32 blocks.

Make 32.

making the rows

1 Arrange eight blocks as shown. Sew together and press the seam allowances open. Make four rows.

Make 4.

2 Sew 16 print rectangles together along their long edges. Press the seam allowances open. Make five rows.

Make 5.

3 Sew the five rectangle rows and four block rows together, alternating them as shown. Press the seam allowances open.

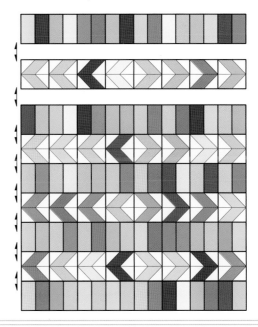

"Kaleidoscope"

| Pieced and quilted by Kate Henderson | Finished quilt: 40" x 44" | Finished block: 4" x 4" |

assembling the quilt

1 Sew a cream strip to each side of the quilt. Press the seam allowances toward the cream border strip. Sew the remaining cream strips to the top and bottom of the quilt. Press the seam allowances toward the border.

2 Referring to "Flying-Geese Units" on page 13, use two cream squares and a print rectangle to make a flying-geese unit as shown. Press the seam allowances open. Make 38.

Make 38.

3 Sew 10 flying-geese units together to make a side border; make two. Press the seam allowances open. Sew nine flying-geese units together for the top border; add a cream square to each end. Press the seam allowances open. Repeat to make the bottom border.

4 Sew the side borders to the quilt and press the seam allowances toward the inner border. Sew the top and bottom borders to the quilt and press the seam allowances toward the inner border.

finishing the quilt

1 Layer the quilt top, batting, and backing; baste the layers together. Quilt as desired. I quilted vertical lines of serpentine stitch using a walking foot.

2 Referring to "Binding" on page 17, use the green strips to bind the edges of the quilt. Add a label if desired.

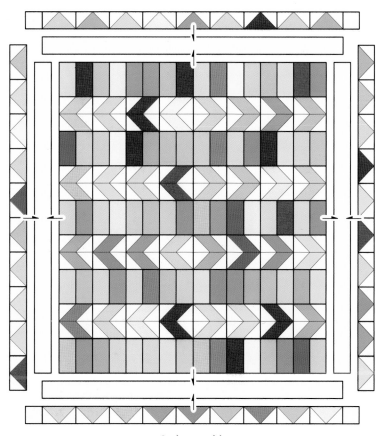

Quilt assembly

wind farm

Pinwheel blocks are among my favorites. I have put them together in groups of four, where they look like little wind farms.

materials

Yardage is based on 42"-wide fabric.

24 fat quarters (18" x 21") of assorted dark prints for the blocks, borders, and binding

2⅜ yards of white solid for blocks, sashing, and borders

4⅝ yards of fabric for backing

60" x 82" piece of batting

cutting

From *each* of the dark-print fat quarters, cut:
5 strips, 2½" x 21"; crosscut into:
  2 strips, 2½" x 19" (48 total)
  1 strip, 2½" x 12" (24 total)
  6 rectangles, 2½" x 4½" (144 total)

From the leftovers of the dark-print strips, cut:
18 different squares, 2½" x 2½"
2 rectangles, 2½" x 4½"

From the white solid, cut:
16 strips, 2½" x 42"; crosscut into 256 squares, 2½" x 2½"
17 strips, 2½" x 42"

making the blocks

1 Organize the 2½" x 19" strips into pairs. Sew the pairs together along their long edges. Press the seam allowances open. Cut each strip set into four squares, 4½" x 4½" (96 total).

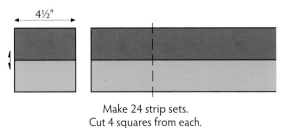

4½"

Make 24 strip sets.
Cut 4 squares from each.

2 Sew together two matching units from step 1 as shown and press the seam allowances open. Make two.

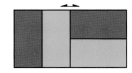

3 Sew together the two units from step 2 and press the seam allowances open. Repeat to make 24 pinwheel units.

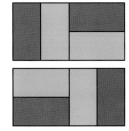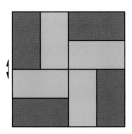

Make 24.

4 Arrange four pinwheel units from step 3 into two rows of two. Sew the units together and press the seam allowances open. Sew the rows together and press the seam allowances open. Repeat to make six block centers.

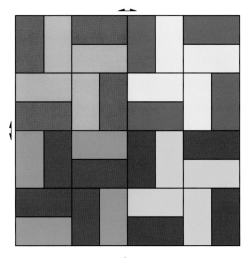

Make 6.

"Wind Farm"

Pieced and quilted by Kate Henderson | **Finished quilt:** 54" x 76" | **Finished block:** 20" x 20"

5 Referring to "Flying-Geese Units" on page 13, use two white squares and a print 2½" x 4½" rectangle to make a flying-geese unit as shown. Press the seam allowances open. Make 96.

Make 96.

6 Sew four flying-geese units together end to end and press the seam allowances open. Make 12; these are side units.

Make 12.

7 Sew four flying-geese units together end to end. Sew a white square to each end of the pieced unit. Press the seam allowances open. Make 12; these are top/bottom units.

Make 12.

8 Sew a side unit to each side of a block center from step 4. Press the seam allowances open. Sew top/bottom units to the top and bottom of the block center and press the seam allowances open. Make six.

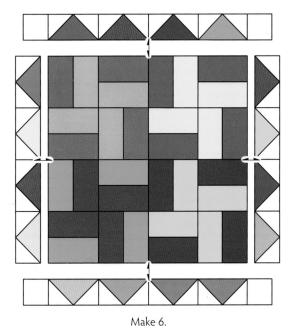

Make 6.

assembling the quilt

1 From two white strips, cut four 2½" x 20½" sashing strips. Sew three blocks and two white sashing strips together, alternating them as shown. Press the seam allowances toward the sashing strips. Make two.

2 Sew five white strips together end to end. From the pieced strip, cut three sashing strips 64½" long. Join the block columns from step 1 with 64½"-long sashing strips on both sides and in the middle. Press the seam allowances toward the sashing strips.

3 Sew three white strips together end to end. From the pieced strip, cut two strips 46½" long. Sew the white 46½"-long strips to the top and bottom of the quilt. Press the seam allowances toward the sashing strips.

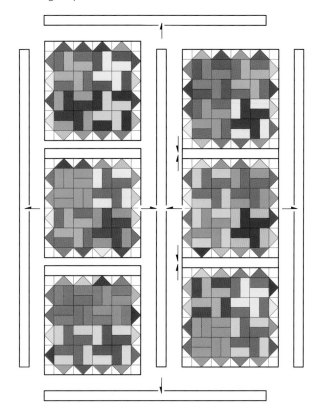

4 Referring to "Triangle Corners" on page 12, use a white square to make a triangle corner at one end of a print 2½" x 4½" rectangle. Make 20 of unit A and 20 of unit B. Press the seam allowances open.

Unit A.
Make 20.

Unit B.
Make 20.

5 Sew six of unit A, six of unit B, three print 2½" x 4½" rectangles, and four print squares together as shown to make a side border. Press the seam allowances open. Make two. Referring to the quilt assembly diagram below, sew a border to each side of the quilt. Press the seam allowances toward the sashing strips.

Make 2.

6 Sew four of unit A, four of unit B, two print 2½" x 4½" rectangles, and five print squares together as shown to make the top border. Press the seam allowances open. Repeat to make the bottom border. Referring to the quilt assembly diagram, sew the borders to the top and bottom of the quilt. Press the seam allowances toward the sashing strips.

Make 2.

7 Sew two white strips together end to end and cut a side border 72½" long; make two. Sew three white strips together end to end. From the pieced strip, cut two strips 54½" long for the top and bottom borders. Sew a 72½"-long strip to each side of the quilt and press the seam allowances toward the white border. Sew 54½"-long strips to the top and bottom of the quilt. Press the seam allowances toward the white border.

finishing the quilt

1 Layer the quilt top, batting, and backing; baste the layers together. Quilt as desired. I free-motion quilted swirls and double loops.

2 Referring to "Scrappy Binding" on page 17, join the 24 print 2½" x 12" strips to make one long strip. Use the pieced strip to bind the edges of the quilt. Add a label if desired.

Quilt assembly

round and round

This pattern looks great in any fabric combination. If you've been wondering how to use a collection of fabrics, this is the project for you.

materials

Yardage is based on 42"-wide fabric.

36 strips, 2½" x 42", of assorted prints for blocks

1⅛ yards of white solid for sashing and borders

½ yard of red print for binding

3¾ yards of fabric for backing

64" x 64" piece of batting

cutting

From *each* of the 36 print strips, cut:
  2 squares, 2½" x 2½" (72 total)
  2 rectangles, 2½" x 4½" (72 total)
  2 rectangles, 2½" x 6½" (72 total)
  1 rectangle, 2½" x 8½" (36 total)

From the white solid, cut:
  3 strips, 2½" x 42"; crosscut into 6 rectangles,
    2½" x 16½"
  3 strips, 2½" x 42"
  6 strips, 3½" x 42"

From the red print, cut:
  6 strips, 2½" x 42"

making the blocks

1 Sew two contrasting print squares together and press the seam allowances open. Sew a 2½" x 4½" rectangle that matches the second square to the unit and press the seam allowances open.

Planning Ahead

It may be helpful to sort the print rectangles into 36 piles, one for each quarter-block unit, before sewing them together. It will be easier to achieve variation within the blocks, and will ensure that matching strips are available when needed.

2 Sew a 2½" x 4½" rectangle of a third print to the side of the unit from step 1. Press the seam allowances open. Sew a matching 2½" x 6½" rectangle to the top of the unit and press the seam allowances open.

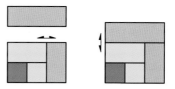

3 Sew a 2½" x 6½" rectangle cut from a fourth print to the side of the unit from step 2. Press the seam allowances open. Sew the matching 2½" x 8½" rectangle to the top and press the seam allowances open. Make 36 quarter-block units.

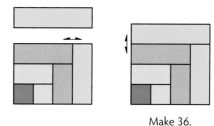

Make 36.

4 Join the quarter-block units together in pairs. Press the seam allowances open. Sew two pairs together to make a block; press. Make nine blocks.

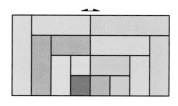

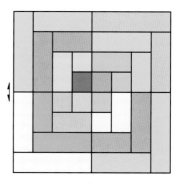

Make 9.

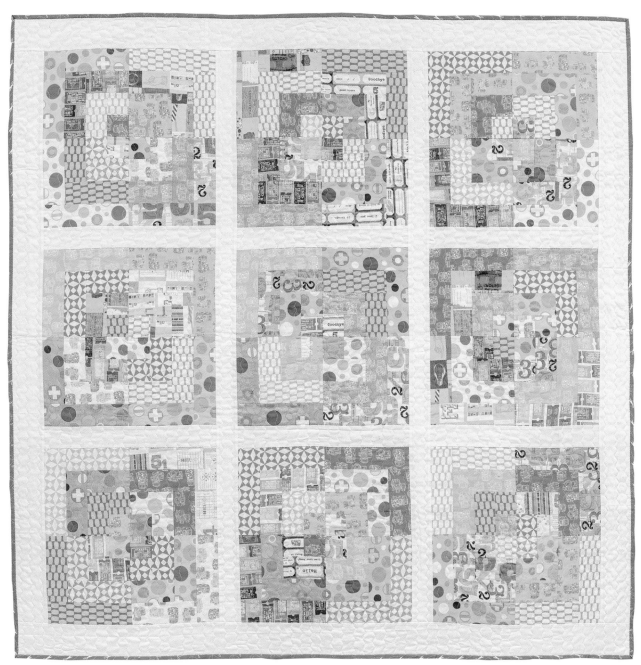

"Round and Round"

Pieced and quilted by Kate Henderson | **Finished quilt:** 58" x 58" | **Finished block:** 16" x 16"

assembling the quilt

1 Sew three blocks and two white 2½" x 16½" rectangles together, alternating them as shown. Press the seam allowances toward the white rectangles. Make three rows.

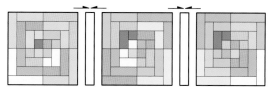

Make 3.

2 Sew the three white 2½" x 42" strips together end to end. From the pieced strip, cut two strips 52½" long.

3 Lay out the assembled rows and 52½"-long sashing strips. Sew together and press the seam allowances toward the sashing strips.

4 Sew three 3½" x 42" white strips together end to end. From the pieced strip, cut two borders 52½" long. Sew the remaining three white strips together end to end; cut two borders 58½" long from the pieced strip.

5 Sew the 52½"-long border strips to the sides of the quilt. Press the seam allowances toward the borders. Sew the 58½"-long border strips to the top and bottom of the quilt. Press the seam allowances toward the borders.

finishing the quilt

1 Layer the quilt top, batting, and backing; baste the layers together. Quilt as desired. I quilted vertical lines of serpentine stitching.

2 Referring to "Binding" on page 17, use the red strips to bind the edges of the quilt. Add a label if desired.

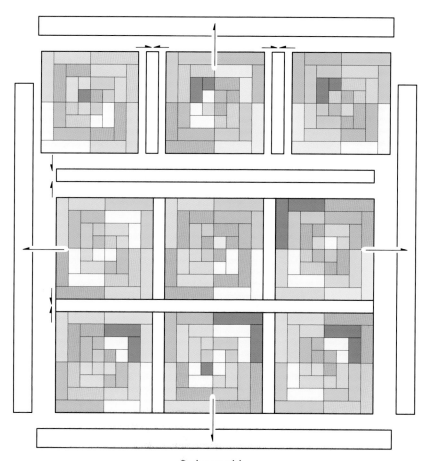

Quilt assembly

little houses

Use some favorite fabrics to make these rows of cute little houses.

materials

Yardage is based on 42"-wide fabric.

67 strips, 2½" x 10", of assorted bright prints for blocks

67 strips, 2½" x 6", of assorted light prints for blocks

1 yard of white solid for background, sashing, and borders

½ yard of red polka dot for binding

3 yards of fabric for backing*

50" x 50" piece of batting

*If your fabric is wide enough, you may be able to use a single panel, in which case you need only 1⅜ yards of backing fabric.

cutting

From *each* of the bright strips, cut:
  2 rectangles, 2½" x 4½" (134 total)

From *each* of the light strips, cut:
  2 squares, 2½" x 2½" (134 total)

From the white solid, cut:
  1 strip, 2½" x 42"; crosscut into 6 rectangles, 2½" x 4½"
  11 strips, 2½" x 42"

From the red polka dot, cut:
  5 strips, 2½" x 42"

making the blocks

1 Referring to "Flying-Geese Units" on page 13, use two matching light squares and a bright rectangle to make a flying-geese unit. Press the seam allowances open. Make 67 using a different bright print for each unit.

Make 67.

2 Sew a matching bright rectangle to the bottom of each unit. Press the seam allowances open. Make 67 blocks.

assembling the quilt

1 Arrange 10 House blocks with the roofs pointing in one direction and sew the blocks together to form a row. Press the seam allowances open. Make four rows.

Make 4.

"Little Houses"

| Pieced and quilted by Kate Henderson | **Finished quilt:** 44" x 44" | **Finished block:** 4" x 4" |

2 Arrange nine House blocks with the roofs pointing in the opposite direction. Add a white 2½" x 4½" rectangle to each end of the row and sew the pieces together. Make three rows.

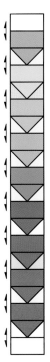

Make 3.

3 Sew three white 2½" x 42" strips together end to end. From the pieced strip, cut two borders 44½" long. From each of the remaining white strips, cut a strip 40½" long.

4 Arrange the rows from steps 1 and 2 and the eight white 40½"-long strips, alternating them as shown. Sew the rows and strips together, pressing the seam allowances toward the sashing and border strips. Sew the 44½"-long strips to the top and bottom of the quilt. Press the seam allowances toward the border strips.

finishing the quilt

1 Layer the quilt top, batting, and backing; baste the layers together. Quilt as desired. I free-motion quilted scrolls and circles in rows.

2 Referring to "Binding" on page 17, use the red polka-dot strips to bind the edges of the quilt. Add a label if desired.

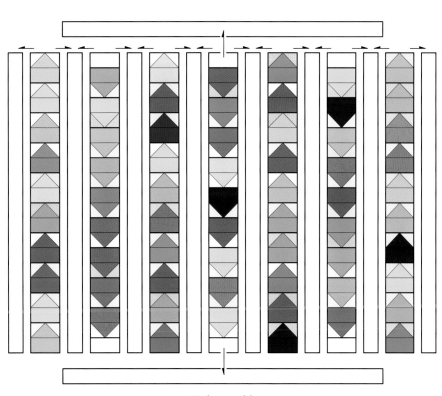

Quilt assembly

Borderless Quilts

Some quilt designs are self-contained and need no borders to make them visually complete. When the top is pieced, the project is ready to layer and quilt.

butterflies

ocean waves

color-block coins

fly away home

fireworks

stepping up

night sky

that '70s quilt

scrappy crosses

steps

reflections

butterflies

There is nothing happier than seeing butterflies fluttering around the garden. Bring the happiness inside and have butterflies fluttering about your house with this quilt.

materials

Yardage is based on 42"-wide fabric.

38 strips, 2½" x 42", of assorted prints for blocks

2⅓ yards of white solid for blocks

⅝ yard of pink print for binding

3⅞ yards of fabric for backing

66" x 66" piece of batting

cutting

From *each* of 25 print strips, cut:
2 rectangles, 2½" x 12½" (50 total)
1 rectangle, 2½" x 10½" (25 total)

From *each* of 13 print strips, cut:
4 rectangles, 2½" x 8½" (52 total; 2 will be left over)

From the white solid, cut:
19 strips, 2½" x 42"; crosscut into:
100 rectangles, 2½" x 4½"
100 squares, 2½" x 2½"
20 strips, 1½" x 42"; crosscut into:
50 rectangles, 1½" x 12½"
50 rectangles, 1½" x 2½"

From the pink print, cut:
7 strips, 2½" x 42"

making the blocks

1 Referring to "Triangle Corners" on page 12, use two white squares to add a triangle to each end of a print 2½" x 12½" rectangle. Press the seam allowances open. Make two from matching print rectangles.

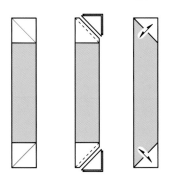

2 Place a white 2½" x 4½" rectangle at right angles on a print 2½" x 8½" rectangle, right sides together. Draw a diagonal line from corner to corner across the overlapped area. Stitch and trim as for "Triangle Corners." Repeat with a second white rectangle at the other end of the print rectangle. Be sure the seam lines are oriented as shown. Press the seam allowances open. Make two from matching print rectangles.

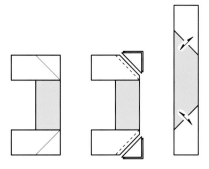

3 Sew a white 1½" x 2½" rectangle to each end of a print 2½" x 10½" rectangle. Press the seam allowances open.

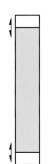

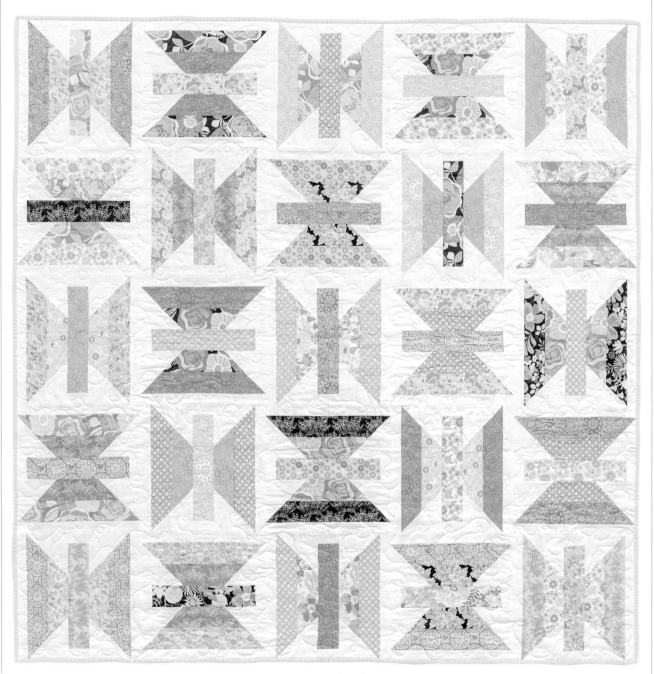

"Butterflies"

Pieced and quilted by Kate Henderson | **Finished quilt:** 60" x 60" | **Finished block:** 12" x 12"

4 Arrange the units from steps 1, 2, and 3 as shown and sew together. Press the seam allowances open. Sew a white 1½" x 12½" rectangle to each side of the block and press the seam allowances toward the white rectangles. Make 25 blocks.

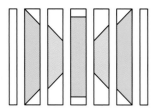 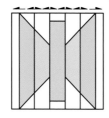

Make 25.

assembling the quilt

1 Arrange the blocks in five rows of five blocks each, rotating every other block as shown in the quilt assembly diagram. Sew the blocks together in rows, pressing the seam allowances toward the white rectangles.

2 Sew the rows together. Press the seam allowances in one direction.

finishing the quilt

1 Layer the quilt top, batting, and backing; baste the layers together. Quilt as desired. I free-motion quilted loops and swirls.

2 Referring to "Binding" on page 17, use the pink strips to bind the edges of the quilt. Add a label if desired.

Quilt assembly

ocean waves

I've used these simple blocks to suggest a wave pattern, but they can be positioned to create many different quilts. Once you've made the blocks, position and rotate them until you find a pleasing arrangement.

materials

Yardage is based on 42"-wide fabric.

36 strips, 2½" x 42", of assorted dark prints for blocks

1¾ yards of cream solid for blocks

⅝ yard of blue solid for binding

3⅞ yards of fabric for backing

66" x 66" piece of batting

cutting

From *each* of the 36 print strips, cut:

1 rectangle, 2½" x 10½" (36 total)

1 rectangle, 2½" x 8½" (36 total)

1 rectangle, 2½" x 6½" (36 total)

1 rectangle, 2½" x 4½" (36 total)

1 square, 2½" x 2½" (36 total)

From the cream solid, cut:

23 strips, 2½" x 42"; crosscut into:

36 rectangles, 2½" x 8½"

36 rectangles, 2½" x 6½"

36 rectangles, 2½" x 4½"

36 squares, 2½" x 2½"

From the blue solid, cut:

7 strips, 2½" x 42"

making the blocks

1 Sew a cream square to one end of each print 2½" x 8½" rectangle; a cream 2½" x 4½" rectangle to one end of each print 2½" x 6½" rectangle; a cream 2½" x 6½" rectangle to one end of each print 2½" x 4½" rectangle; and a cream 2½" x 8½" rectangle to one side of each print square. Press all the seam allowances open.

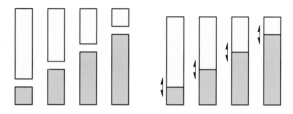

2 Join four pieced units made with a single print and the matching 2½" x 10½" rectangle as shown to make a block. Press all the seam allowances open. Make 36 blocks.

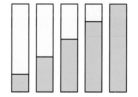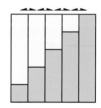

Make 36.

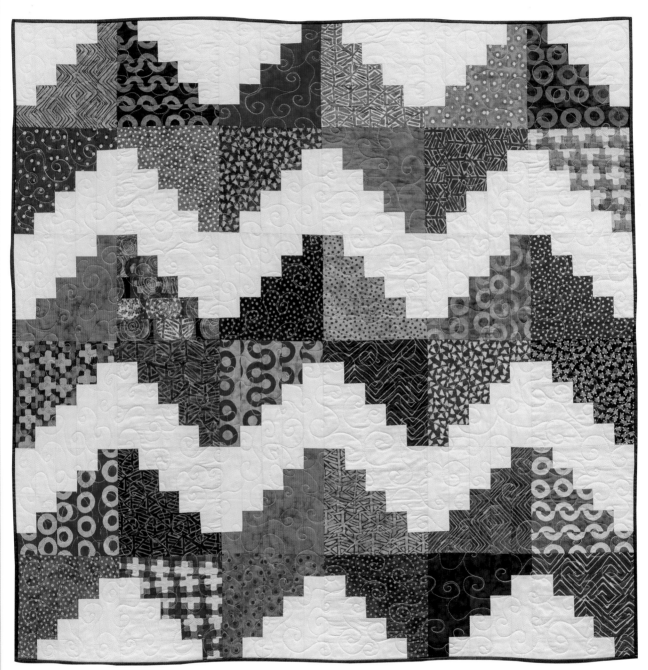

"Ocean Waves"

Pieced and quilted by Kate Henderson | **Finished quilt:** 60" x 60" | **Finished block:** 10" x 10"

assembling the quilt

1 Arrange the blocks in six rows of six blocks each. Rotate alternating blocks to make a wave pattern as shown in the quilt assembly diagram, or arrange as desired. Sew the blocks together in rows and press the seam allowances open.

2 Sew the rows together. Press the seam allowances open.

finishing the quilt

1 Layer the quilt top, batting, and backing; baste the layers together. Quilt as desired. I free-motion quilted an all-over wave pattern.

2 Referring to "Binding" on page 17, use the blue strips to bind the edges of the quilt. Add a label if desired.

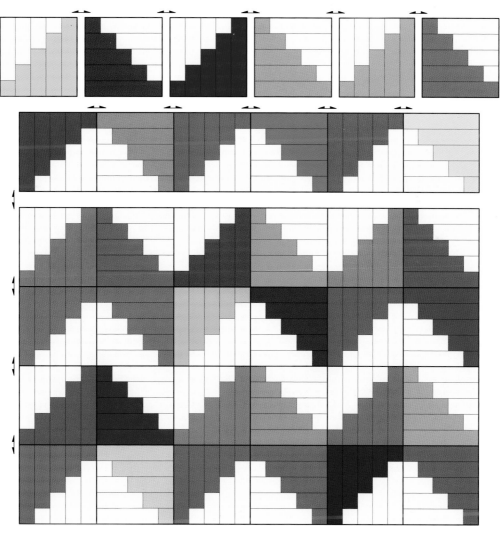

Quilt assembly

color-block coins

Looking at color-block dresses inspired this simple Coin quilt. I think this design would also look great in shades of just one color.

materials

Yardage is based on 42"-wide fabric.

10 strips, 2½" x 42", of fabric in *each* of four color families for piecing and binding

½ yard of white solid for background

2¾ yards of fabric for backing*

46" x 50" piece of batting

If your fabric is wide enough, you may be able to use a single panel, in which case you need only 1½ yards of backing fabric.

Strip Option

I used a Jelly Roll to provide lots of different fabrics for my quilt, but it can be made with just 20 strips: five each of four different colors. Cut four rectangles, 2½" x 8½", from each strip. You'll also need ½ yard of fabric for a one-fabric binding.

cutting

Sort the strips into four color families; I used gray, red, blue, and green.

From the 10 strips of *each* color family, cut:
    20 rectangles, 2½" x 8½" (80 total)

Keep the remainder of each strip to make the binding.

From the white solid, cut:
    3 strips, 4½" x 40½"

making the rows

Position the 20 rectangles of one color family in a pleasing arrangement. Sew the rectangles along their long edges to make a row. Press the seam allowances open. Make four rows.

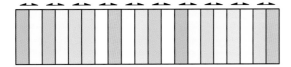

Press all seam allowances open.

assembling the quilt

1 Lay out the pieced rows and white strips, alternating them as shown in the quilt assembly diagram.

2 Sew the rows and strips together. Press the seam allowances toward the white strips.

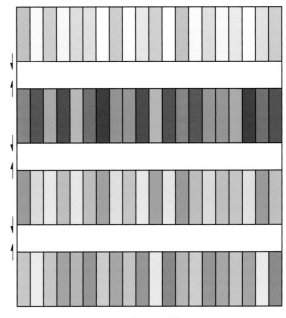

Quilt assembly

finishing the quilt

1 Layer the quilt top, batting, and backing; baste the layers together. Quilt as desired. I free-motion quilted an all-over pattern of circles.

2 Referring to "Scrappy Binding" on page 17, join the leftover pieces from the 2½" colored strips to make a single strip at least 180" long. Use the pieced strip to bind the edges of the quilt. Add a label if desired.

"Color-Block Coins"

Pieced and quilted by Kate Henderson

Finished quilt: 40" x 44"

fly away home

I love the secondary pattern created by the geese flying toward and away from the square blocks in this quilt.

materials

Yardage is based on 42"-wide fabric.

40 strips, 2½" x 42", of assorted pastel prints for blocks

2 yards of white solid for blocks

½ yard of orange print for binding

3⅔ yards of fabric for backing

60" x 60" piece of batting

cutting

From *each* of 36 print strips, cut:
  2 squares, 2½" x 2½" (72 total)
  3 rectangles, 2½" x 4½" (108 total)
  2 rectangles, 2½" x 6½" (72 total)

From *each* of 3 print strips, cut:
  2 squares, 2½" x 2½" (6 total)
  4 rectangles, 2½" x 4½" (12 total)
  2 rectangles, 2½" x 6½" (6 total)

From the remaining print strip, cut:
  4 squares, 2½" x 2½" (4 total)
  4 rectangles, 2½" x 6½" (4 total)

From the white solid, cut:
  18 strips, 2½" x 42"; crosscut into 281 squares, 2½" x 2½"
  14 strips, 1½" x 42"; crosscut into 80 rectangles, 1½" x 6½"

From the orange print, cut:
  6 strips, 2½" x 42"

making the square blocks

1 Sew matching print squares to the top and bottom of a white square. Press the seam allowances toward the print squares.

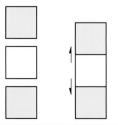

2 Sew matching print 2½" x 6½" rectangles to both sides of the unit from step 1. Press the seam allowances toward the print rectangles. Make 41 blocks.

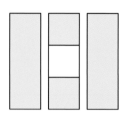
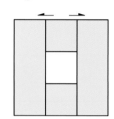

Make 41.

making the flying geese blocks

1 Referring to "Flying-Geese Units" on page 13, use two white squares and a print 2½" x 4½" rectangle to make a flying-geese unit. Press the seam allowances open. Make 120 units.

2 Sew three flying-geese units together as shown. Press the seam allowances open.

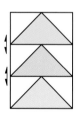

3 Sew a white 1½" x 6½" rectangle to each side of the unit from step 2. Press the seam allowances toward the white rectangles. Make 40 blocks.

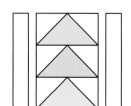
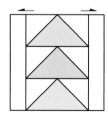

Make 40.

"Fly Away Home"

Pieced and quilted by Kate Henderson

Finished quilt: 54" x 54"

Finished block: 6" x 6"

assembling the quilt

1 Arrange the blocks in nine rows of nine blocks each, alternating Square and Flying Geese blocks as shown in the quilt assembly diagram. Pay attention to the direction of the flying-geese units in each block. Sew the blocks together in rows, pressing the seam allowances toward the Square blocks.

2 Sew the rows together. Press the seam allowances in one direction.

finishing the quilt

1 Layer the quilt top, batting, and backing; baste the layers together. Quilt as desired. I free-motion quilted a pattern of overlapping triangles.

2 Referring to "Binding" on page 17, use the orange strips to bind the edges of the quilt. Add a label if desired.

Quilt assembly

fireworks

This quilt, made up in bright prints, reminds me of fireworks exploding in the sky.

materials

Yardage is based on 42"-wide fabric.

36 strips, 2½" x 42", of assorted bright prints for blocks

1⅞ yards of white solid for blocks

⅝ yard of blue print for binding

3¼ yards of fabric for backing

57" x 74" piece of batting

cutting

From *each* of the 36 print strips, cut:
1 strip, 2½" x 27" (36 total)

From the leftovers of 12 print strips, cut:
12 squares, 2½" x 2½"

From the white solid, cut:
6 strips, 2½" x 42"; crosscut into:
  24 rectangles, 2½" x 6½"
  24 squares, 2½" x 2½"
3 strips, 9¾" x 42"; crosscut into 12 squares,
  9¾" x 9¾". Cut the squares into quarters diagonally to yield 48 triangles.
3 strips, 5⅛" x 42"; crosscut into 24 squares,
  5⅛" x 5⅛". Cut the squares in half diagonally to
  yield 48 triangles.

From the blue print, cut:
7 strips, 2½" x 42"

making the blocks

1 Sew white 2½" squares to opposite sides of a print 2½" square. Press the seam allowances open.

2 Sew white 2½" x 6½" rectangles to the top and bottom of the unit from step 1. Press the seam allowances open. Make 12 units.

3 Organize the print 2½" x 27" strips into 12 piles of three strips each. Sew each group of strips together along their long edges. Press the seam allowances open. Cut each strip set into four squares, 6½" x 6½" (48 total).

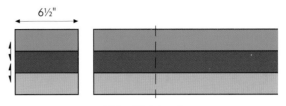

Make 12 strip sets.
Cut 4 squares from each.

4 Arrange a unit from step 2, four matching units from step 3, four half-square triangles (corners), and four quarter-square triangles (top, bottom, and sides) as shown to make a block. Sew into diagonal rows and press the seam allowances open. Sew the rows together and press the seam allowances open. Make 12 blocks.

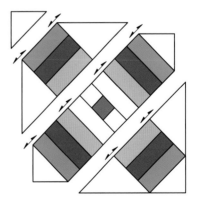

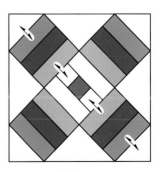

Make 12.

"Fireworks"

Pieced and quilted by Kate Henderson	**Finished quilt:** 51" x 68"	**Finished block:** 17" x 17"

assembling the quilt

1 Arrange the blocks in four rows of three blocks each. Sew the blocks together in rows and press the seam allowances open.

2 Sew the rows together. Press the seam allowances open.

finishing the quilt

1 Layer the quilt top, batting, and backing; baste the layers together. Quilt as desired. I free-motion quilted swirls and flowers.

2 Referring to "Binding" on page 17, use the blue strips to bind the edges of the quilt. Add a label if desired.

Quilt assembly

stepping up

Use bold colors and prints for this modern take on a traditional Courthouse Steps block.

materials

Yardage is based on 42"-wide fabric.

42 strips, 2½" x 42", of assorted dark prints for blocks

21 strips, 2½" x 42", of assorted light solids for blocks

⅝ yard of black print for binding

3⅞ yards of fabric for backing

66" x 76" piece of batting

cutting

From *each* of the dark-print strips, cut:
  1 square, 2½" x 2½" (42 total)
  2 rectangles, 2½" x 6½" (84 total)
  2 rectangles, 2½" x 10½" (84 total)

From *each* of the 21 light-solid strips, cut:
  4 squares, 2½" x 2½" (84 total)
  4 rectangles, 2½" x 6½" (84 total)

From the black print, cut:
  7 strips, 2½" x 42"

making the blocks

1 Sew matching solid 2½" squares to the top and bottom of a print 2½" square. Press the seam allowances open.

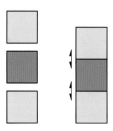

2 Sew matching print 2½" x 6½" rectangles to both sides of the unit from step 1. Press the seam allowances open.

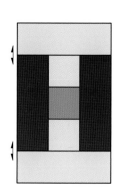

3 Sew matching solid rectangles to the top and bottom of the unit from step 2. Press the seam allowances open.

4 Sew matching print 2½" x 10½" rectangles to both sides of the unit from step 3. Press the seam allowances open. Make 42 blocks.

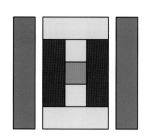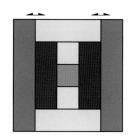

Make 42.

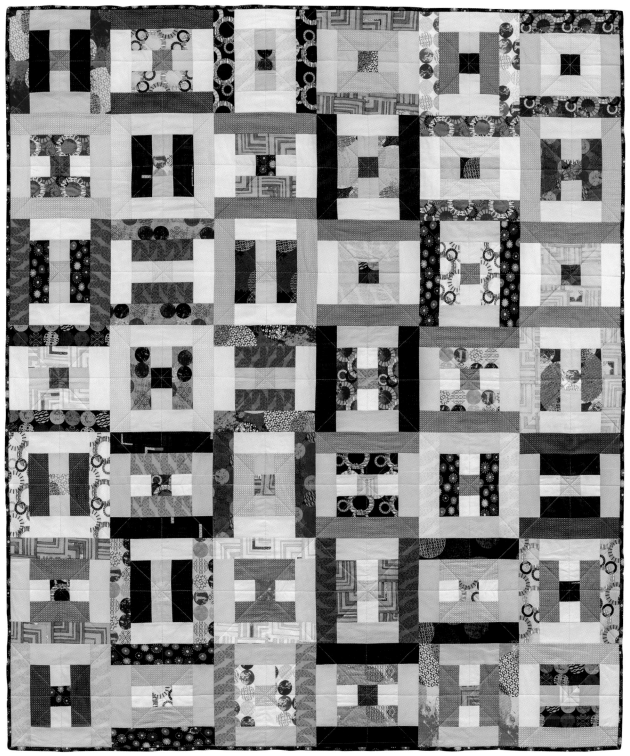

"Stepping Up"

Pieced and quilted by Kate Henderson | **Finished quilt:** 60" x 70" | **Finished block:** 10" x 10"

assembling the quilt

1 Arrange the blocks in seven rows of six blocks each, rotating every other block as shown. Sew the blocks together in rows and press the seam allowances open.

2 Sew the rows together. Press the seam allowances open.

finishing the quilt

1 Layer the quilt top, batting, and backing; baste the layers together. Quilt as desired. I quilted vertical, horizontal, and diagonal straight lines to form an asterisk in the center of each block.

2 Referring to "Binding" on page 17, use the black strips to bind the edges of the quilt. Add a label if desired.

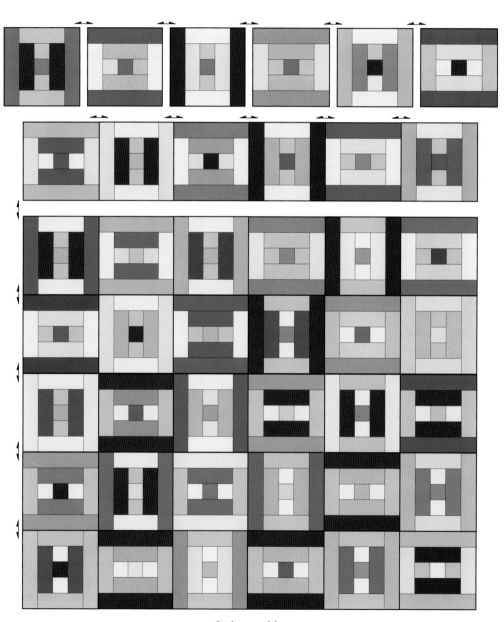

Quilt assembly

night sky

Bright prints really pop against a dark background, making the stars in this quilt twinkle.

materials

Yardage is based on 42"-wide fabric.

51 strips, 2½" x 42", of assorted bright prints for blocks

3⅞ yards of dark-gray solid for background

¾ yard of red print for binding

4¼ yards of fabric for backing

72" x 72" piece of batting

Optional: 45° Half-Square Triangle ruler by Creative Grids

cutting

From *each* of 31 print strips, cut:
   4 squares, 2½" x 2½" (124 total)
   4 rectangles, 2½" x 6½" (124 total)
   Each strip will make 2 Planet blocks; the pieces for 1 block will be left over.

From *each* of the remaining 20 print strips, cut:
   15 squares, 2½" x 2½" (300 total)
   Each strip will make three Star blocks.

From the dark-gray solid, cut:
   50 strips, 2½" x 42"; crosscut into 785 squares, 2½" x 2½"
   If your fabric is too narrow to cut 16 squares per strip, cut up to three additional strips before crosscutting.

From the red print, cut:
   8 strips, 2½" x 42"

Half-Square Triangles

Using the 45° Half-Square Triangle ruler to cut the half-square triangles can save time and fabric. If you use this method, cut 545 gray 2½" squares from 35 strips and three 2½" squares from *each* of the 20 print strips chosen for the Star blocks. Cut the remaining strips with the ruler to assemble the half-square triangle units.

To cut the half-square triangles, place a gray strip and a print strip right sides together, matching the edges carefully. Place the ruler on top and follow the manufacturer's instructions to cut 12 pairs of half-square triangles. Sew them together and press the seam allowances open.

making the planet blocks

1 Referring to "Triangle Corners" on page 12, use a gray square to make a triangle corner at each end of a print rectangle. Press the seam allowances open. Make two matching units.

2 Sew matching print squares to opposite sides of a gray square. Press the seam allowances open.

3 Sew the units from step 1 to the top and bottom of the unit from step 2 as shown. Press the seam allowances open. Make 61.

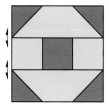

Make 61.

making the star blocks

1 Referring to "Half-Square-Triangle Units" on page 13, make a half-square-triangle unit using one print and one gray square. Press the seam allowances open. Make four matching units.

"Night Sky"

| Pieced and quilted by Kate Henderson | **Finished quilt:** 66" x 66" | **Finished block:** 6" x 6" |

2 Sew gray squares to both sides of a half-square-triangle unit from step 1, orienting the half-square-triangle unit as shown. Press the seam allowances open. Make two matching units.

3 Sew matching half-square-triangle units from step 1 to both sides of a print square, orienting the half-square-triangle units as shown. Press the seam allowances open.

4 Sew the units from step 2 to the top and bottom of the unit from step 3 as shown. Press the seam allowances open. Make 60.

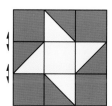

Make 60.

assembling the quilt

1 Arrange the blocks in 11 rows of 11 blocks each, alternating the Planet and Star blocks. Sew the blocks together in rows and press the seam allowances open.

2 Sew the rows together. Press the seam allowances open.

finishing the quilt

1 Layer the quilt top, batting, and backing; baste the layers together. Quilt as desired. I free-motion quilted swirling lines and stars.

2 Referring to "Binding" on page 17, use the red strips to bind the edges of the quilt. Add a label if desired.

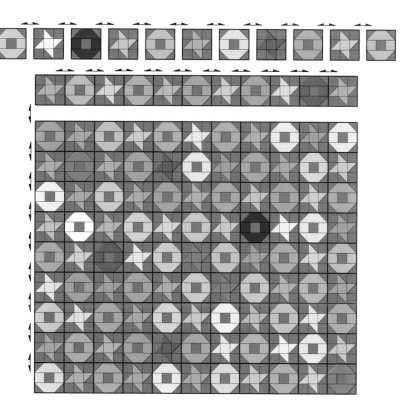

Quilt assembly

that'70s quilt

Turning a simple block on point gives it a completely new look.

materials

Yardage is based on 42"-wide fabric.

38 strips, 2½" x 42", of assorted bold prints for blocks

3 yards of white solid for background

¾ yard of black print for binding

4⅜ yards of fabric for backing

74" x 74" piece of batting

cutting

From *each* of 25 print strips, cut:
    2 rectangles, 2½" x 10½" (50 total)
    2 rectangles, 2½" x 6½" (50 total)
    2 squares, 2½" x 2½" (50 total)

From *each* of 13 print strips, cut:
    4 rectangles, 2½" x 6½" (52 total; 2 will be left over)
    5 squares, 2½" x 2½" (65 total)

From the white solid, cut:
    24 strips, 2½" x 42"; crosscut into:
        64 rectangles, 2½" x 10½"
        100 squares, 2½" x 2½"
    2 strips, 15⅜" x 42"; crosscut into 3 squares, 15⅜" x 15⅜". Cut the squares into quarters diagonally to yield 12 triangles.
    1 strip, 8" x 42"; crosscut into 2 squares, 8" x 8". Cut the squares in half diagonally to yield 4 triangles.

From the black print, cut:
    8 strips, 2½" x 42"

making the blocks

1. Sew matching print squares to the top and bottom of a contrasting print square. Press the seam allowances open.

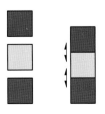

2. Sew 2½" x 6½" rectangles that match the outer squares to both sides of the unit from step 1. Press the seam allowances open.

3. Sew matching 2½" x 6½" rectangles that contrast with the rest of the block to the top and bottom of the unit from step 2. Press the seam allowances open.

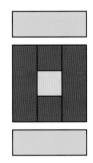
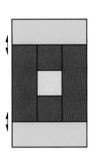

4. Referring to "Triangle Corners" on page 12, use white squares to make a triangle corner at each end of a print 2½" x 10½" rectangle. The rectangle should match those added in step 3. Press the seam allowances open. Make two matching units.

5. Sew the units from step 4 to both sides of the unit from step 3, orienting the triangles as shown. Press the seam allowances open. Make 25.

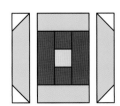
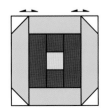

Make 25.

"That '70s Quilt"

Pieced and quilted by Kate Henderson | **Finished quilt:** 68" x 68" | **Finished block:** 10" x 10"

assembling the quilt

1 Trim 16 of the remaining print squares ¼" from the diagonal centerline of the square as shown. This is similar to the trimming for triangle corners on page 12.

2 Arrange the blocks, white rectangles, setting triangles, remaining print squares, and trimmed squares from step 1 as shown in the quilt assembly diagram. Sew the pieces together into diagonal rows. Press the seam allowances open.

3 Sew the rows together. Press the seam allowances open.

finishing the quilt

1 Layer the quilt top, batting, and backing; baste the layers together. Quilt as desired. I free-motion quilted a meandering pattern.

2 Referring to "Binding" on page 17, use the black strips to bind the edges of the quilt. Add a label if desired.

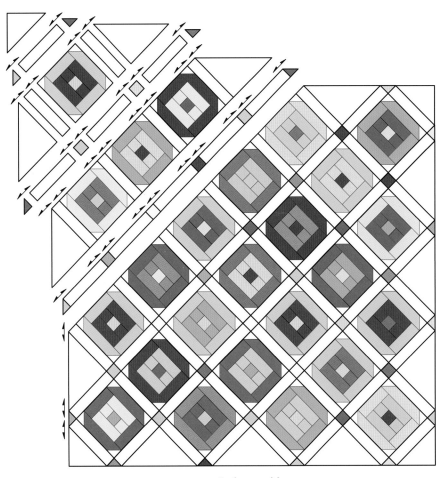

Quilt assembly

scrappy crosses

*I love to make a few scrappy Cross blocks when I have a little spare time.
If you do the same, you'll have enough for a quilt top before you know it.*

materials

Yardage is based on 42"-wide fabric.

Scraps at least 2½" x 12" of 40 or more assorted prints OR 1⅜ yards *total* for blocks and binding

⅓ yard *each* of 7 different solids for blocks

2⅞ yards of fabric for backing*

46" x 56" piece of batting

If your fabric is wide enough, you may be able to use a single panel, in which case you need only 1⅝ yards of backing fabric.

cutting

From *each* of the 7 different solids, cut:
   1 strip, 10" x 42"; crosscut into 3 squares,
      10" x 10" (21 total; 1 will be left over)

From the scraps, cut:
   20 strips, 2½" x 10"
   20 strips, 2½" x 11½"
   2½"-wide strips of various lengths, totaling at
      least 200"

Seemingly Solid

For the solid fabrics, you can substitute shot cottons (as I did) or tone-on-tone prints that read as solids from a distance.

making the blocks

1 Cut a solid square horizontally no less than 2" from the top or bottom edge; variation between blocks is acceptable and adds variety in the quilt. Sew a print 2½" x 10" strip between the two pieces. Press the seam allowances toward the print strip.

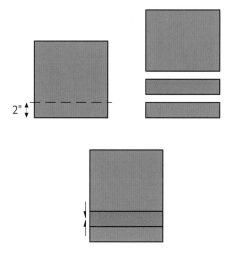

2 Cut the unit from step 1 vertically no less than 2" from one side edge. Sew a print 2½" x 11½" strip between the two pieces. Press the seam allowances toward the print strip. Trim the block to measure 10½" x 10½". Make 20 blocks.

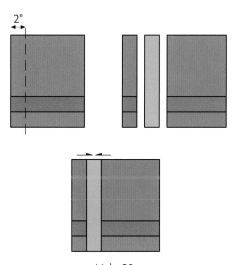

Make 20.

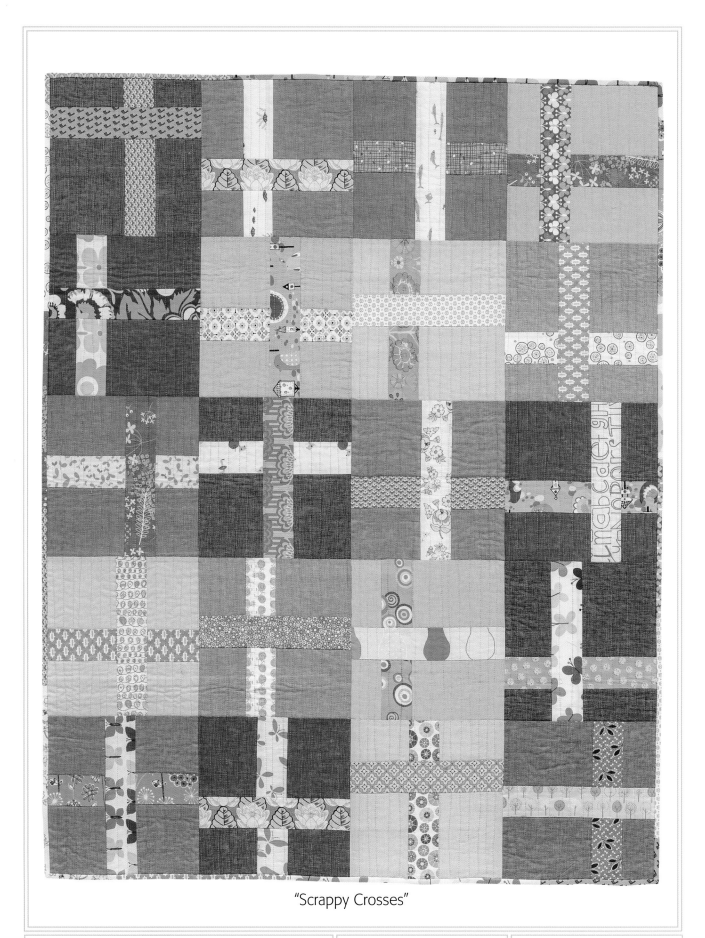

"Scrappy Crosses"

| Pieced and quilted by Kate Henderson | **Finished quilt:** 40" x 50" | **Finished block:** 10" x 10" |

assembling the quilt

1 Arrange the blocks in five rows of four blocks each, rotating the crosses as desired. Sew the blocks together in rows, pressing the seam allowances in alternating directions from row to row.

2 Sew the rows together. Press the seam allowances in one direction.

finishing the quilt

1 Layer the quilt top, batting, and backing; baste the layers together. Quilt as desired. I quilted straight vertical lines using a walking foot.

2 Referring to "Scrappy Binding" on page 17, join the assorted scraps of 2½" strips to make a strip at least 190" long. Use the pieced strip to bind the edges of the quilt. Add a label if desired.

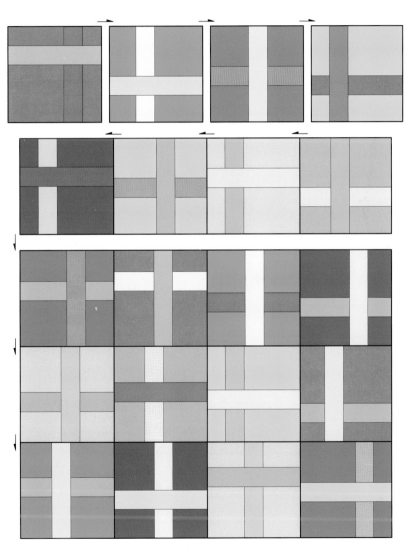

Quilt assembly

steps

Collect all your favorite 2½" x 4½" scraps to make this quilt. Once you've made all the blocks, play around with the quilt layout. There are so many different quilts you can make with this simple little block.

materials

Yardage is based on 42"-wide fabric.

64 rectangles, 2½" x 4½", of assorted prints for blocks

⅔ yard of white solid for blocks

⅜ yard of yellow polka dot for binding

1⅛ yards of fabric for backing

38" x 38" piece of batting

cutting

From the white solid, cut:
8 strips, 2½" x 42"; crosscut into 64 rectangles, 2½" x 4½"

From the yellow polka dot, cut:
4 strips, 2½" x 42"

making the blocks

Sew a print rectangle to a white rectangle to make a square. Press the seam allowances toward the print.

Make 64.

assembling the quilt

1 Arrange the blocks in eight rows of eight blocks each, rotating the blocks as shown, or see "Alternate Layout" on page 74. Sew the blocks together in rows, pressing the seam allowances in alternating directions from row to row.

2 Sew the rows together. Press the seam allowances in one direction.

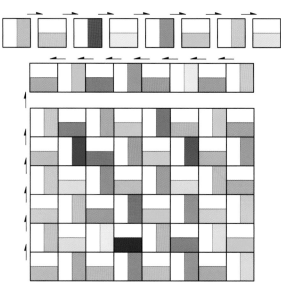

Quilt assembly

finishing the quilt

1 Layer the quilt top, batting, and backing; baste the layers together. Quilt as desired. I quilted straight vertical lines one inch apart.

2 Referring to "Binding" on page 17, use the yellow polka-dot strips to bind the edges of the quilt. Add a label if desired.

"Steps"

Pieced and quilted by Kate Henderson   **Finished quilt:** 32" x 32"   **Finished block:** 4" x 4"

Alternate Layout

I made a second "Steps" quilt without the steps. I used my favorite pieces of screen-printed linen and cotton with an aqua background fabric, and rotated the blocks in every other row 180°.

An alternate layout for "Steps" blocks

reflections

I never tire of red and aqua no matter how many times I use them together. This quilt's black-print background really makes the colors pop.

materials

Yardage is based on 42"-wide fabric.

40 strips, 2½" x 42", of assorted red and aqua prints for blocks

3⅝ yards of black print for background and binding

4¼ yards of fabric for backing

73" x 84" piece of batting

45°-triangle ruler at least 8½" tall (such as the Large Kaleido-Ruler by Marti Michell) OR template plastic

cutting

From the black print, cut:
8 strips, 8½" x 42"
22 strips, 2½" x 42"

making the rows

1 Organize the assorted red and aqua print strips into 10 strip sets of four strips each. Sew each strip set together along their long edges. Press the seam allowances open.

Make 10 strip sets.

2 Place the prepared template on one strip set, aligning the blunted point with one long raw edge of the fabric and the base of the triangle with the opposite raw edge. Trace along the template's angled edges and cut. Rotate the template 180° and position it next to the angled cut edge, making sure the top and bottom of the triangle align with the fabric edges.

Cut a second triangle. Repeat to cut eight triangles from each strip set (80 total).

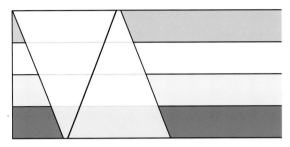

Cut 8 from each, 80 total.

3 Remove the selvages from a black 8½" x 42" strip and fold the strip in half, matching the raw edges. Position the template on a folded strip, aligning the top and bottom edges as before, and positioning the guideline along the cut ends of the strip. Cut along the angled edge of the template to make two half triangles. Continue cutting the fabric strip to make four pairs of full triangles, rotating the template 180° each time. Unfold the remainder of the strip and cut one more triangle. Repeat with the other black 8½" x 42" strips. You will have 16 half triangles (eight pairs) and 72 full triangles.

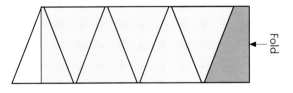

Fold

Cutting Triangles

To make the quilt without using a specialty ruler, trace the pattern on page 78 onto template plastic and cut out. Be sure to trace the guideline near the center of the triangle onto the template. Lay the template on the assembled strip sets or strips as directed, mark the angled lines onto the fabric, and cut along the lines. Use scissors, or lay a rotary-cutting ruler along the line and cut with a rotary cutter.

To use the Large Kaleido-Ruler, position the blunted tip of the ruler's 45° triangle on one raw edge of the fabric, with the 8½" line on the opposite raw edge. Cut along the angled edges of the ruler. When cutting the half triangles, align the dotted line to the left of the ruler's center with the ends of the fabric strip.

"Reflections"

Pieced and quilted by Kate Henderson

Finished quilt: 66¼" x 78"

4 Arrange 10 strip-set triangles and nine black triangles into a row. Add a half triangle at each end and sew the triangles together. Press all the seam allowances open. Make eight.

Make 8 rows.

assembling the quilt

1 Sew two black 2½" x 42" strips together end to end. Press the seam allowances open and cut a 66¾"-long sashing strip. Make seven.

2 Arrange the triangle rows and sashing strips as shown. Sew the rows and sashing strips together. Press the seam allowances toward the sashing strips.

finishing the quilt

1 Layer the quilt top, batting, and backing; baste the layers together. Quilt as desired. I quilted vertical straight lines.

2 Referring to "Binding" on page 17, use the remaining eight black strips to bind the edges of the quilt. Add a label if desired.

Quilt assembly

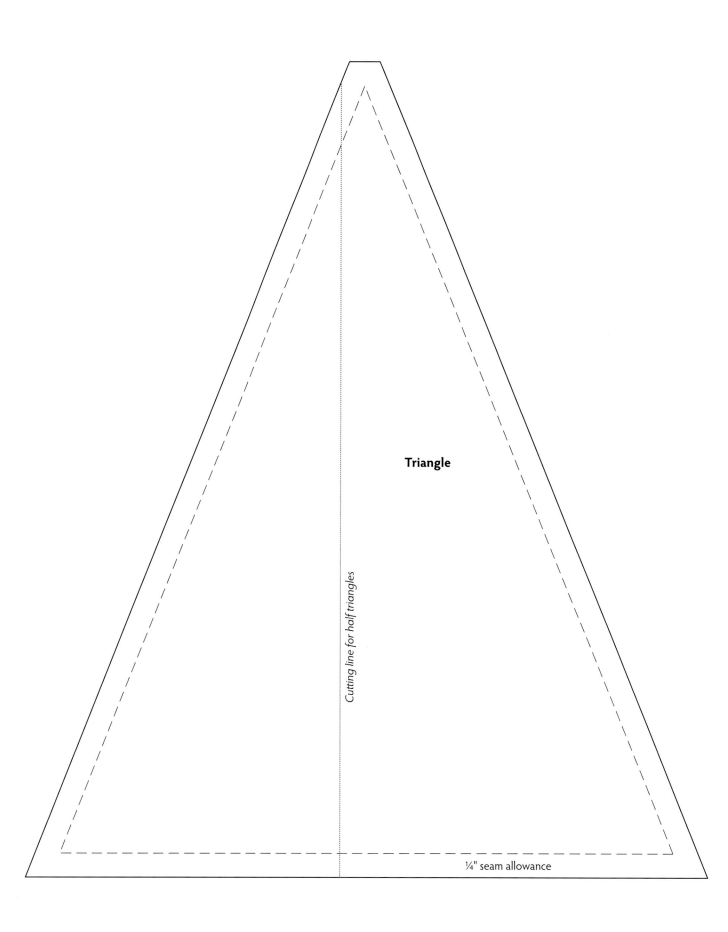

Triangle

Cutting line for half triangles

¼" seam allowance

acknowledgments

The chance to write this book came just as I was having my fourth child and there is no way I could even have contemplated doing it without my incredibly encouraging and supportive husband, Chris.

Thanks to my grandmother Noma, who instilled in me a love of beautiful fabrics, design, and sewing.

Thanks to everyone at Martingale who encouraged me to write this book.

Thanks to Moda for the beautiful Jelly Rolls used in these projects.

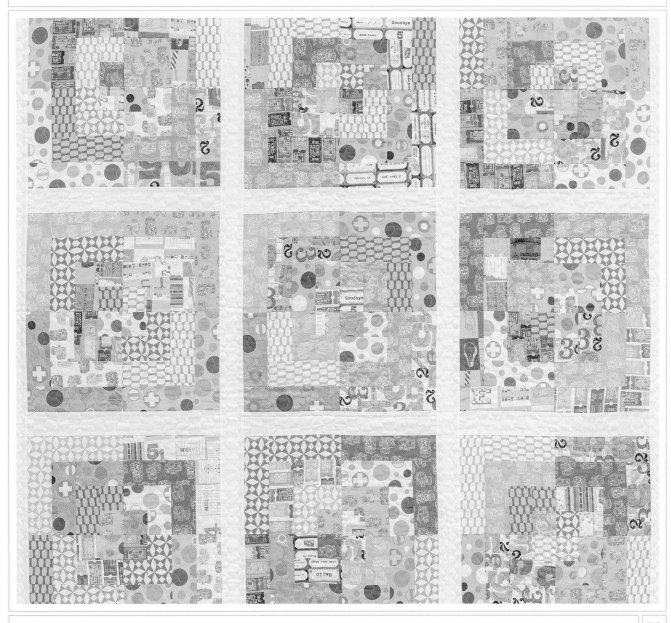

about the author

Kate learned to sew clothes at the age of 12 and has sewn for herself ever since. After her twins were born in 2005, she began designing soft toys for them and to sell as a way to stay sane while her babies were little. Soon she began selling patterns for those toys and the quilts she was making.

She has never met a fiber craft she doesn't like and when she isn't sewing, she likes knitting and spinning. If she could sneak a loom or long-arm quilting machine into the house unnoticed, she would.

Kate lives in the southwest of Western Australia with her husband and four girls. She blogs about her crafting adventures and her life at TwoLittleBanshees.com.